Francis Holland School

R17105

weblinks

You don't need a computer to use this book. But, for readers who do have access to the Internet, the book provides links to recommended websites which offer additional information and resources on the subject.

You will find weblinks boxes like this on some pages of the book.

weblinks

For more information about military intervention go to
www.waylinks.co.uk
/EthicalDebates/
militaryintervention

waylinks.co.uk

To help you find the recommended websites easily and quickly, weblinks are provided on our own website, **waylinks.co.uk.** These take you straight to the relevant websites and save you typing in the Internet address yourself.

Internet safety

↗ Never give out personal details, which include: your name, address, school, telephone number, email address, password and mobile number.

↗ Do not respond to messages which make you feel uncomfortable – tell an adult.

↗ Do not arrange to meet in person someone you have met on the Internet.

↗ Never send your picture or anything else to an online friend without a parent's or teacher's permission.

↗ If you see anything that worries you, tell an adult.

A note to adults
Internet use by children should be supervised. We recommend that you install filtering software which blocks unsuitable material.

Website content

The weblinks for this book are checked and updated regularly. However, because of the nature of the Internet, the content of a website may change at any time, or a website may close down without notice. While the Publishers regret any inconvenience this may cause readers, they cannot be responsible for the content of any website other than their own.

WAYLAND

Military Intervention

KAYE STEARMAN

WAYLAND

First published in 2007 by Wayland
Reprinted in 2007

Copyright © Wayland 2007

Wayland
338 Euston Road
London NW1 3BH

Wayland Australia
Level 17/207 Kent Street
Sydney, NSW 2000

Editor: Patience Coster
Series Editor: Camilla Lloyd
Consultant: Tom Woodhouse
Designer: Rita Storey
Picture Researcher: Diana Morris

Picture Acknowledgements: The author and
publisher would like to thank the following for
allowing their pictures to be reproduced in
this publication:
Cover photograph: A UN peacekeeper is
surrounded by Congolese children
in Bukara, Democratic Republic of Congo
(MONUC/Handout/Corbis)
John Berry/Syracuse Newspapers/Image
Works/Topfoto: 1, 19, AP/Topfoto: 5, 21, 28, 34,
35, Photri/Topham: 6, Dimitri Beliakov/Rex
Features: 7, Sipa Press/Rex Features: 8, 14b, 27,
40, Picturepoint/ Topham: 9, 11, 13, 14t, 30,
The British Library/The Art Archive: 10,
Topfoto: 12, Patrick Chauvel/Sygma/Corbis: 15,
MONUC/Reuters/Corbis: front cover, 16,
UN/Topham: 17, Tony O'Brien/Image
Works/Topfoto: 20, Bob Daemmrich/Image
Works/Topfoto: 23, William Karel/Sygma
/Corbis: 24, Andy Holbrooke/The Image
Works/Topfoto: 29, Reuters/Corbis: 31, Peter
Macdiarmid/MOD Pool/Topfoto: 32, Armando
Babani/EPA/Corbis: 33, Louise Gubb/Image
Works/Topfoto: 36, Tony Savino/Image
Works/Topfoto: 37, Hubert Boesl/DPA/Corbis:
38, Emmanuel Braun/Reuters/Corbis: 39, Sabah
Arar/Rex Features: 41, Rawan/Rex Features: 42,
Peter Turnley/Corbis: 43, Thorne
Anderson/Corbis: 44.

The author gives thanks to the organisations
and websites who supplied information for
this book, especially those covering UN
peacekeeping operations, *The Human Scarcity
Report 2005* and the Institute of War and Peace
Reporting.

British Library Cataloguing in
Publication Data
Stearman, Kaye
  Military intervention. - (Ethical debates)
  1. Intervention (International Law) -
  Moral and ethical aspects -
  Juvenile literature
  I. Title
  172.4'2

ISBN: 978 0 7502 5028 3

Printed in China

Wayland is a division of Hachette Children's
Books, an Hachette Livre UK Company.

contents

Introduction
Real-life case study 4

Chapter 1
What is military intervention? 6

Chapter 2
The reasons for military intervention 12

Chapter 3
Defending national security 18

Chapter 4
Intervening to keep the peace 24

Chapter 5
Intervening to prevent disaster 28

Chapter 6
When there is no intervention 34

Chapter 7
The costs of intervention 40

Glossary 46

Timeline 47

Further information 47

Index 48

Real-life case study

This case study highlights some of the issues that surround the debate on military intervention.

case study

No safe havens in Bosnia

In 1991, the once-unified country of Yugoslavia broke apart. The result was Europe's longest and most violent conflict since the Second World War. The worst affected country was Bosnia-Herzegovina, where there was fierce fighting between different ethnic groups and intervention by militias from neighbouring Croatia and Serbia.

The ferocity of the conflict and the fear that it could spread further prompted the world, in the form of the United Nations (UN) to intervene. The United Nations is an organization that was set up at the end of the Second World War, with the aim of preventing future wars. Today more than 190 nations belong to the UN.

In February 1991, the United Nations Protection Force (UNPROFOR) was established to protect so-called 'safe haven' areas of Croatia. In 1992, the UN mandate was extended to Bosnia to ensure the delivery of humanitarian aid and to protect refugees. Altogether, 39 countries contributed almost 39,000 soldiers to UNPROFOR.

The UN peacekeepers faced an immense task. Bosnia was a small country, but the mountainous terrain and harsh winters meant that communications and transport were difficult. There was fighting on many fronts, with cities under siege, shifting alliances and broken ceasefires. Civilians were deliberately targeted, killed, tortured and driven from their homes in a type of persecution that became known as 'ethnic cleansing'. Hundreds of thousands of people were on the move, living in camps or bombed-out buildings.

Sarajevo, Bosnia's capital, had once been a vibrant city where people of different religions and ethnic backgrounds lived side by side. Now it became a dangerous and divided place. From April 1992, Serbian-backed forces blockaded the city, cutting off sources of food and medicine, water, gas and electricity. Their forces controlled the surrounding hills and trained their guns on the people below. They pounded Sarajevo with heavy mortar fire, reducing buildings to rubble. Every day people were killed and injured, but it was impossible to escape because the Serbs had also laid mines in the surrounding mountains.

One of the first tasks of UNPROFOR was to negotiate the reopening of Sarajevo airport. Under UN protection, food and medicines reached destitute people and a few were able to leave for safer areas. UNPROFOR also agreed to extend its protection to safe havens – isolated areas now surrounded by enemy troops – such as Srebrenica. In co-operation with NATO forces, UNPROFOR also operated 'no-fly zones' to stop aerial bombing of civilians.

However, as the situation deteriorated so did the authority of the UN troops. Their role was essentially a peacekeeping and humanitarian one, and they lacked sufficient troop numbers and resources to do more. When the UN tried to negotiate ceasefires or disarm participants, their representatives were attacked and kidnapped. Meanwhile, the city of Sarajevo remained under siege. Women and children were routinely killed as they queued for food or water. Many of those who had welcomed the UN peacekeepers became increasingly bitter at their inability to protect civilians or stop the fighting.

In June 1995, the safe haven of Srebrenica was invaded by Bosnian Serbian troops. The UNPROFOR battalion of Dutch troops based in Srebrenica failed to protect the terrified civilian population. As a result, more than 8,000 men and boys were massacred by the Bosnian Serbs and women and girls were sent into exile.

The Bosnian war came to an end in December 1995, when increased NATO military action and international pressure forced a negotiated settlement. The siege of Sarajevo did not end until February 1996. For the UN, Bosnia had been a bitter and frustrating experience. Despite their achievements, it seemed that UNPROFOR had not been properly able to protect the suffering and destitute victims of war. Rather, Bosnia set the stage for new thinking about how to improve the effectiveness of UN peacekeeping.

It's a fact

The majority of people killed in conflicts today are civilians, not soldiers.

▼ Russian peacekeepers acting under the UN mandate with Bosnian Serbs in Pale, close to the Bosnian capital, Sarajevo, in February 1994.

CHAPTER 1

What is military intervention?

Military intervention, for many reasons, is one of the most controversial issues in the world today. It raises fundamental questions about how countries relate to one another, and whether there are situations in which it is right for one country to send armed forces into another country.

One reason the subject is so difficult is because it is so wide-ranging. There are many types of intervention, and each draws a range of opposition and support. In particular, the US-led invasion of Iraq in March 2003 divided world opinion – including opinions within the United Nations itself. Yet, nine years earlier, the UN had been severely criticized for not taking military action in the African country of Rwanda, to stop the genocide of almost a million people. (Genocide means a deliberate attempt to wipe out an entire group of people.) So is military intervention justified – and if so, when and how?

Different views

For some people, the question is straightforward. Pacifists, people who oppose any violence on religious or moral grounds, believe that military intervention is always wrong. They say that there is always a peaceful solution to international tensions, and that the only response to military force is non-violent resistance.

Other groups believe that military intervention should only be used as the very last option, when all other possibilities have been exhausted. When a country is behaving unethically, whether by breaking international laws or mistreating its citizens, then non-military pressure should be applied. This may include diplomatic isolation, such as denying visas to

▼ Soldiers on guard duty near a burning oil-well during the US-led invasion of Iraq in 2003.

▲ A Russian tank passes through the bombed-out wasteland that is Grozny, the capital city of Chechnya. The war in Chechnya has been fought with great brutality on all sides.

weblinks

For more information about working to prevent and resolve deadly conflicts, go to www.waylinks.co.uk/Ethical Debates/ militaryintervention

government officials. Or it may involve cutting economic aid or imposing international sanctions by, for example, refusing to trade with the country in question. Groups who believe in this approach argue that military force kills innocent civilians, destroys the economy and creates new problems for countries that are already in crisis.

Other groups believe that military intervention can be used positively, to enforce international laws, prevent mass killing or keep the peace. Supporters say that, in these situations, urgent and decisive intervention by armed forces acting with the full authority of the UN is the only solution. Once safety and security have been restored through the use of military intervention, then people can return to other methods of resolving tensions.

On the other hand, some groups strongly support unilateral military intervention – military action by one country against another. For example, a prominent group in US politics known as the neo-conservatives (or 'neo-cons') believes that the world is threatened by 'rogue states' – countries that support terrorism. Neo-cons say that these rogue states will not respond to normal diplomatic pressure or to the UN. They argue that military intervention is therefore necessary for US (and world) security. Neo-cons say that if the UN will not act, then the USA should act alone.

▲ Preparing for genocide – Hutu recruits training with wooden rifles in Kigali, the capital of Rwanda, in 1994. Some people argue that forceful military intervention in Rwanda (see pages 34-6) might have helped prevent the killings.

While some people support or oppose military intervention as a moral issue, others see it as a pragmatic one. This means that they see it as a question of judgement, depending on the specific situation. They believe it is possible to weigh up whether or not there is a good reason for intervention, to work out what the costs will be in life and resources, and to assess whether intervention will achieve its goals. Of course, much depends on the way in which people are involved – especially if they are citizens or soldiers of the countries concerned – and how the intervention affects their lives.

Intervention or invasion?

So what do we mean by the term 'military intervention'? Many people would define it as similar to 'war' or 'invasion by a foreign army'. War is a violent conflict between the armies of two or more countries. Civil war describes a situation in which different groups within a country are at war with one another. Wars range from huge conflicts involving dozens of countries and resulting in massive loss of life (as in the First and Second World Wars) to border clashes between neighbouring countries, resulting in limited casualties.

Military intervention is a particular type of war. It is sometimes called 'police action' or 'humanitarian intervention' or a 'peacekeeping operation', although each of these terms describes a particular sort of military intervention.

What are the main differences between a war and a military intervention? In a war there is normally a formal 'declaration of war'; this is not the case in a military intervention. Some military interventions are secretive, and are often carried out by guerrilla armies funded by outsiders. However, a UN peacekeeping operation has to be approved by the UN Security Council, usually after much discussion and debate.

A war is a conflict between countries. A military intervention is where one country (or group of countries) sends armed forces to enter and occupy another country, without similar action on the other side. Military intervention is mainly carried out by large and powerful countries against smaller countries. It rarely happens the other way round.

War is open-ended, no one knows how long it will last and normally it continues until one side is victorious and the other formally surrenders. A military intervention has a specific objective (political, economic, humanitarian) and aims to be temporary, although in practice it may become open-ended and last for many years.

weblinks↖

For more information about humanitarian assistance and protection for refugees, go to www.waylinks.co.uk/EthicalDebates/ militaryintervention

It's a fact

There has been no period of open warfare between major world powers since 1945 – some historians refer to our era as the 'long peace'. However, there have been many 'small wars' and political violence, especially in Africa, Asia and the Middle East.

The UN peacekeeping force in ▶ Cyprus was established in 1964 to maintain peace between Turkish and Greek Cypriots.

One of the most brutal military campaigns in history was led by Genghis Khan, a Mongolian leader in the twelfth century. His nomadic (roving) army conquered huge areas of Asia and the Middle East.

Why intervene?

Wars and military interventions have been recorded throughout history. In fact, there are many examples in history where war has been the driving force that transforms small but determined societies into major economic and political powers. Military interventions have enabled countries to consolidate power, crush uprisings and punish rebels.

However, other justifications for interventions have been put forward. They include economic reasons, such as the need to exploit new lands and resources, to expand markets and secure trade routes. There have also been religious reasons for interventions, including the need to defeat or destroy other religions, to promote a certain set of beliefs and convert others to follow those beliefs. Political arguments have been used, including the need to secure and expand the intervening country's political power over other countries. And security reasons have been used, such as the need to stop invaders and to secure and expand the intervening country's borders.

Today, countries always prefer to say that they intervene for moral or humanitarian reasons, rather than selfishly to extend their economic or political power. However, critics say that the underlying motives of countries are always to support their national interests, especially if they are large and powerful countries capable of gathering support from the UN and other international bodies.

Since the 1990s, there has been greater pressure for the UN and other international organizations to intervene for humanitarian reasons, either to prevent or limit disaster, such as famine or genocide, or to keep warring peoples apart and support a peaceful solution. Many of these military interventions are controversial, and not all have been successful. Some people believe the intervening nations use moral arguments in order to make economic or political power grabs.

But supporters argue that we can no longer stand by and let millions of innocent people suffer if intervention will save lives. However, in a world where countries can easily plunge into warfare, it is likely that there will be more military interventions for humanitarian reasons.

summary

▶ Military intervention is when one country sends armed forces into another country.

▶ There are many different reasons why a country might intervene militarily in another country – including economic expansion, political domination, promoting religious or other belief systems, and protecting its own security.

▶ In recent years, there have been 'humanitarian' interventions; they include those involving international peacekeeping and preventing disaster or genocide.

▼ Intervening to exploit new territories: Portuguese explorers land at the Bay of Porto Seguro on the coast of Brazil in 1500. Explorers to the New World often used military power to overcome opposition from indigenous peoples.

CHAPTER 2

The reasons for military intervention

Conflicts between and within countries have occurred throughout history. According to the *Human Security Report 2005*, there were 199 international wars and 251 civil wars between the years 1816 and 2002. Historian Eric Hobsbawm says that 187 million people died in wars in the twentieth century alone.

Why have there been so many wars?

In the nineteenth and early twentieth centuries there were many colonial wars. These took place when European countries invaded and conquered areas of Africa and Asia, at first defeating the indigenous inhabitants, and later one another. The main objective of this type of military intervention was to gain access to the precious resources these continents had to offer.

The colonizing countries then took control of the trade routes and channelled a steady stream of wealth back to Europe. When local peoples in Africa and Asia rebelled, the European countries used their military might to crush them.

The Cold War

In 1945, at the end of the Second World War, a new organization, the United Nations, came into being. Its aim was to foster peace between nations and human rights for all. In reality the world was not peaceful. Europe's colonial empires were crumbling. Some colonies gained independence peacefully, but many had to fight violent 'wars of liberation', often followed by equally violent civil wars.

The Cold War (1945-89) was a period during which the two major world powers of the time – the communist East and the capitalist West – were intensely suspicious of and hostile towards each other. On the one side, in the communist countries (which included the

◀ British troops land in Egypt during the 'Suez crisis' of 1956 (see page 13). However, international and Egyptian opposition forced them to withdraw shortly afterwards.

▲ Soviet tanks in the streets of Budapest, the capital of Hungary, in 1956. More than 2,000 Hungarians died as a result of Soviet intervention and 200,000 fled the country as refugees.

It's a fact

In most of today's conflicts, hunger and disease created by war conditions kill more people than missiles, bombs and bullets.

Soviet Union and China), political and economic power lay in the hands of the state, which was controlled by the Communist Party. On the other side, the West (which included the USA, Western Europe, Canada and Japan) supported capitalist economics and political parties competing for power. In practice, things were not quite so simple. The Soviet Union and China were soon fighting over their borders and there were tensions between the USA and its allies.

In October 1956, there were two major military interventions. British and French forces, together with Israel, invaded Egypt after the Egyptian government had announced it would take over ownership of the Suez Canal, the major trade route for the oil industry. Although the invasion was successful, the USA refused to give its support, saying that the British and French were fighting an old-fashioned colonial war. The invading armies agreed to withdraw their forces, overseen by the first UN peacekeeping force.

Meanwhile, in Europe, the Hungarian people rose in protest against the Soviet Union's domination of their country. The Soviets sent in their army to bring Hungary back into line and the protest was brutally crushed by Soviet troops. The countries involved in both military interventions claimed that they had acted to protect assets vital to their economic and political security. However, many people saw such conflicts as part of the Cold War.

▲ Equipped by the West: in 1954, Carlos Castillo Armas (in the centre), an anti-communist leader in Guatemala, Central America, received US military support to overthrow the elected government. He became president of Guatemala and ruled as a dictator.

Proxy wars

During the Cold War, the political powers competed to supply aid, trade and weapons to the newly independent developing countries. In African and Asian countries, what became known as 'proxy wars' (wars fought by one country on another country's behalf) saw armies equipped with the latest weapons fighting to support the political or economic interests of their military backers. In Central America, the US government supported 'coups' against elected governments. It backed guerrilla armies in their attempts to attack and undermine governments that had policies of which the USA did not approve.

It's a fact

Military coups, where the army overthrows the government to take power for itself, were common in the twentieth century. In 1963 alone there were 25 coups and attempted coups. In 2004, there were only ten coup attempts and all of them failed.

weblinks↖

For more information about facts and figures on conflicts worldwide, go to
www.waylinks.co.uk/EthicalDebates/
militaryintervention

In 1989, the Cold War suddenly ended. The Soviet Union lost its power over Eastern Europe and began to fall apart. Proxy wars and open military intervention became much less common. Why was this?

Some supporters of military intervention, such as the neo-cons in the USA, say the world is more peaceful today because the USA was prepared to use military intervention to defend its interests against the spread of communism. By doing so,

they say, it helped bring about the collapse of the Soviet Union and an end to the Cold War. The Soviets see it differently, however, and would argue that the huge cost of military intervention placed such a strain on the Soviet Union that it contributed to its collapse.

It's a fact

At the beginning of the twenty-first century, more people were being killed in wars in Africa than in the rest of the world combined.

▼ Equipped by the Soviets: MPLA soldiers in Angola, southern Africa, in 1975. Angola was continuously at war from 1975 to 1989, then again from 1992 to 2002. As a result, the country has been devastated.

Democractic Republic of Congo – the child soldier's story

For five years (1998-2003), several African armies and numerous militias fought over the territory of the Democratic Republic of Congo (DRC). The DRC (formerly called Zaire) is Africa's largest country and one of the richest in resources, although most people live surrounded by extreme poverty and corruption.

The war started with a power struggle between the DRC government and the Rwandan army, which had occupied parts of eastern DRC. Soon there was outright warfare, with the DRC government, supported by troops from Zimbabwe, Angola and Namibia on one side, and Rwanda, Uganda and Burundi on the other. There were also many dangerous and undisciplined local militias, like the RCD-Goma, who roamed the countryside, killing and looting at will.

Millions of people were caught up in the fighting, which was brutal on all sides. One of these was Paul, from the Kasai region in eastern DRC. He tells his story: 'I was 13 when I was recruited by the RCD-Goma in 1999. They used to come to our village and beat people up. One day they came to our house and took everything we had. So I decided to join them so that nobody could come and beat us up any more.'

'In Kasai we fought the Zimbabwean soldiers. In 2001 I was moved to Minembwe to fight against Masunzu's forces. Later, the Rwandans decided to take all of us off to Rwanda so that we wouldn't join Masunzu's forces. They told us we were going to be trained in Rwanda, but when we arrived we were put in prison for five months. There were about 500 of us. We were kept in chains and were sometimes beaten. Afterwards we were brought back to Bukavu – an RCD-Goma official negotiated our return. I am still not in contact with my family.'

A United Nations report accused the intervening countries of economic exploitation of DRC's rich mineral resources. While a few people became wealthy, the outcome was a humanitarian disaster. At least 3.3 million people died, some in conflict, but most as a result of famine, malnutrition and disease – the highest death toll since the Second World War. Thousands of women and girls were raped, millions fled their homes, and schools and hospitals were destroyed. Children like Paul are still forced to fight against their will.

A peace agreement was signed in 2002, monitored by a United Nations peacekeeping force called MONUC. However, in many areas violence and lawlessness continue. Meanwhile, the lure of DRC's wealth may tempt outsiders into further military interventions.

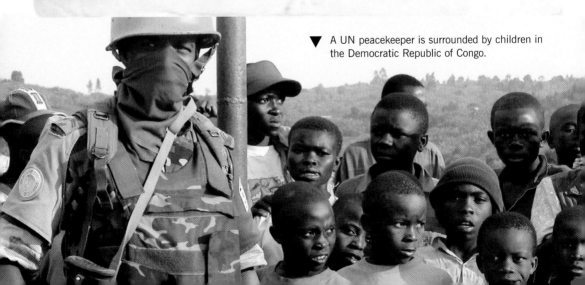

▼ A UN peacekeeper is surrounded by children in the Democratic Republic of Congo.

Opponents of military intervention say that Cold War intervention was far from beneficial. They believe it contributed to a more violent world, keeping alive political divisions that might otherwise have healed. In particular, they point to the effect of military interventions in countries where governments are weak or undemocratic. In a world awash with weapons, many smaller and poorer nations have equipped themselves with arms and are prepared to fight for resources.

Continuing conflicts

The *Human Security Report* says that today we are witnessing a dramatic decrease in international and civil wars, with far fewer deaths during conflicts. However, violence has increased in one continent. Since 1989, over 90 per cent of deaths in conflict have been in Africa, where there have been many 'small wars'. By and large, these wars have attracted little coverage by the media. Many are civil wars, while others have been fought across the artificial borders created by colonial rule, often backed by outside powers. Whatever the causes, the results have been disastrous, with huge numbers of people killed, injured and starved amid destruction and collapse.

It's a fact

According to the charity Save the Children, around 300,000 children, some as young as seven years of age, are fighting in wars around the world today.

v i e w p o i n t s

'You have to make war to have peace. We are preparing to return our forces to the DRC.'
Paul Kagame, president of Rwanda, speaking to United Nations peacekeeping forces, 23 November 2004

'Sexual violence is a national epidemic in DRC, involving all military factions, both current and past military forces involved in the internal affairs of the DRC, and it appears to be sanctioned by all levels of military command.'
Survivors' Rights International, 5 December 2004

summary

► Wars and conflicts have occurred throughout history.

► During the Cold War, great powers often used military intervention to maintain their power; this type of intervention included proxy wars in developing countries.

► After the end of the Cold War proxy wars became less common, but conflicts continue, especially in Africa.

► Young boys and girls have been conscripted into rebel armies in Sierra Leone and other African countries.

CHAPTER 3

Defending national security

▲ Planes hijacked by members of al-Qaeda fly into the World Trade Center in New York on 11 September 2001.

Today people no longer find it acceptable for a country to declare that it will use military intervention to build an empire, as it did in colonial times, or to protect assets or support a particular political system, as happened during the Cold War. Now other reasons are given to support military intervention. One of these is that it is needed to support national security and act against terrorism.

Terrorism is the use of political violence by a country or organization against civilians and, ultimately, their governments. It is often presented as a new threat to world security, but it has been around for many years. The *Human Security Report 2005* says that between 1975 and 2005 terrorist attacks killed around 1,000 people a year

It's a fact

On 7 August 1998, 257 people were killed and more than 4,000 wounded in simultaneous al-Qaeda suicide car bomb explosions at US embassies in the African cities of Nairobi and Dar Es Salaam.

worldwide, and the number of major terrorist attacks has risen steeply in recent years. Most attacks take place in civil wars and conflicts in South Asia and the Middle East and involve car bombs exploding in streets and markets, killing and injuring civilians. Other attacks are aimed at soldiers. Only a small number of terrorist attacks are international incidents.

In the first decade of the twenty-first century, the USA and its allies declared a 'war on terror'. They have given this as their reason for intervening militarily in the countries of Afghanistan and Iraq. Russia gives similar reasons for its military intervention in Chechnya, a small Muslim republic in the Caucasus Mountains, many of whose citizens have been fighting for independence from Russia. Today terrorism, particularly 'Islamic terrorism', is presented as a threat to governments and to world security as a whole.

Al-Qaeda

On 11 September 2001, two aircraft crashed into the World Trade Center in New York City and another aircraft was flown into the Pentagon building in Washington DC. Together they killed almost 3,000 innocent people. The attacks became known simply as 9/11, and were the first foreign attacks to take place on US soil since the Second World War. They were soon discovered to have been the work of an organization called al-Qaeda, based in Afghanistan in central Asia.

With a wealthy and charismatic Saudi-born leader called Osama bin Laden, the al-Qaeda organization has been in existence for several years. It has bombed military and civilian targets in several countries, causing considerable loss of life. Al-Qaeda follows strict Islamic rules – although many Muslims do not agree with their interpretation – and claims that its attacks are *jihad* ('holy war') against countries responsible for suppressing Muslims in Palestine, Iraq and Saudi Arabia.

The 9/11 attacks caused worldwide revulsion and condemnation in the United Nations. The USA was determined to take action against al-Qaeda. President George W. Bush declared a war on terror. Within a month the USA, with support from its NATO allies, had launched 'Operation Enduring Freedom'. This US-led military intervention consisted of air and ground attacks on al-Qaeda military bases in Afghanistan. Attacks were also made on al-Qaeda's allies, the Taliban, who had taken over the government of Afghanistan. The aim was to hunt down the leaders of al-Qaeda and destroy their hold on Afghanistan.

▼ Following the 9/11 attacks, US troops were sent to Afghanistan to hunt down the al-Qaeda terrorists who were based in the country.

▲ Afghanistan had been involved in a long-running and destructive conflict since 1979. But the war on terror created new casualties, like these men at a Red Cross hospital in Kabul.

viewpoints

'I'm confident the American people understand that when it comes to our security, if we need to act, we will act, and we really don't need United Nations' approval to do so.'
George W. Bush, president of the USA, March 2003

'For powerful countries to adopt a principle of preventative war may well set an example that has catastrophic consequences.'
Former US president Jimmy Carter, in his Nobel Peace Prize speech, 2002

The war on terror

The US military intervention in Afghanistan was very controversial. Supporters claimed that the destruction of al-Qaeda and its Taliban allies was the only way to deal with a dangerous force that had already killed thousands of people. They argued that al-Qaeda was similar to Hitler and the Nazis – and that there could be no compromise. They said that Operation Enduring Freedom would quickly and decisively eliminate al-Qaeda and destroy it forever, thereby defeating terrorism and making the world safer.

However, there were also many critics of the military intervention. Some argued that the use of force was simply wrong, others

that it was disproportionate. They said that sophisticated US weapons, such as cruise missiles and cluster bombs, were being used against guerrilla fighters armed with secondhand weapons left over from past battles. But the main victims of the fighting were innocent civilians. The civilian casualties in Afghanistan are unknown, but the lowest estimate is that at least 1,000 civilians died in the first months of attacks.

Other critics said that the intervention showed little real understanding of the situation. It did not address the issue of why al-Qaeda had been able to operate so freely in Afghanistan or the reasons why some Muslims were prepared to listen to its message. These critics pointed out that the intervention had been largely ineffective – most of the al-Qaeda and Taliban leadership had not been captured, and terrorist attacks continued. And, although there was a new democratically elected government in Afghanistan, it was very fragile and hardly capable of governing a broken and desperately poor country.

'Weapons of mass destruction'

The terrorist attacks of 9/11 had long-term effects. In 2002, the USA declared it feared that Iraq, ruled by the dictator Saddam Hussein, was in a position to launch terrorist attacks. President George W. Bush said the threat from Iraq was so great that the USA needed to take pre-emptive (preventative) action against it. He stated that the Iraqi government had weapons of mass destruction (WMDs).

In the past Saddam Hussein had used WMDs against his enemies, but UN inspectors had been sent to find and destroy them. However, the inspectors faced huge difficulties and Saddam Hussein consistently refused to confirm whether the WMDs had actually been destroyed. The US government argued that Iraq presented a 'growing' threat, not just from the WMDs, but also from al-Qaeda terrorists who were now based in Iraq. British Prime Minister Tony Blair even declared that Iraq possessed missiles that could be fired at the UK and could reach it in 45 minutes.

Critics said that the USA and UK were either deliberately exaggerating or lying about WMDs in order to justify military intervention in Iraq. They said that the evidence for the existence of WMDs was weak and that Iraq presented no threat to the outside world.

Saddam Hussein became president of Iraq in 1979 and ruled ruthlessly until his overthrow in 2003. He was executed in December 2006.

case study

USA – the families' stories

In March 2003, US forces led a massive air and land invasion of Iraq. Within three weeks, the forces had occupied the capital Baghdad and US President George W. Bush declared victory. US casualties were initially low. However, as opposition to the US occupation grew, casualties rose. Three years after the invasion, more than 2,000 US soldiers had been killed.

Within the USA there were many people who passionately supported or opposed the war. But the rising death toll brought the consequences directly into the homes of ordinary Americans.

Eddie Mae's nephew, Brett, died when a civilian fuel truck crashed into his army vehicle. Despite her loss, Eddie Mae says that she supports the US intervention in Iraq. 'I would rather have a president that's tough than one who tries to act nice to our enemy.

There is a price to be paid, and I am proud of Brett and the job he was doing in Iraq.' Arnold, whose 21-year-old son Scott died from horrific burns injuries, is also supportive. He says: 'Mistakes have been made in Iraq but I feel that our government did the best with what information they had and they acted on it. You have to jump sometimes and look back later.'

Others disagree, however. John's son was killed in the opening days of the war, when two US Navy helicopters collided. 'There has been horrific mismanagement of the whole operation in Iraq. Now President Bush is saying that he made some mistakes but you can't turn the clock back and undo those mistakes.' Celeste became a peace activist after her son Jose, a national guardsman, was killed by an explosion in Baghdad. She says that the president should resign. 'We shouldn't have gone to Iraq in the first place, we are not wanted there and we should withdraw our troops before more US soldiers die.'

A disputed intervention

The USA also argued that Saddam Hussein should be removed from power on human rights grounds. As leader of Iraq, Saddam had carried out mass killings, imprisonment and torture of his political opponents. The USA stated that military intervention would rid the Iraqi people of a dictator and enable the election of a democratic government.

Opponents of military intervention argued that in the past the USA had been happy to give Saddam support, including selling him weapons. They said

there were other governments who had developed WMDs or abused human rights, but the USA was not preparing to take action against them. Instead, opponents believed that military intervention was an opportunity for the USA to expand its political power, to control Iraq's rich oil fields and establish US companies in the Iraqi market.

In early 2003, the US government attempted to gain United Nations support for military intervention in Iraq, but failed. The majority of countries said that they were not prepared to back an invasion, as Iraq did not pose an immediate threat. Amid worldwide protest, the US-led invasion went ahead in March 2003, without UN support but with UK government backing.

The invasion was militarily very successful. After a massive bombing campaign, Saddam Hussein's armies were quickly defeated and coalition forces established an uneasy hold over the country. But there had been little long-term planning by the occupiers, and millions of Iraqis found themselves living in squalor without water, sewerage, electricity or medicines. There was also growing resistance against the occupying troops, and the country began to slide into violence and chaos.

summary

► Protecting national security and acting against terrorism are reasons for military intervention.

► Terrorism is often presented as a new threat, but it has been around for many years.

► After the 9/11 attacks on the USA, the US government declared a war on terror and launched a military intervention into Afghanistan and Iraq.

► The Iraq intervention was especially controversial and divided opinion in the USA and the world.

▼ An anti-war rally held in Austin, Texas, in February 2003 – one of the many demonstrations worldwide against the US-led invasion of Iraq.

CHAPTER 4

Intervening to keep the peace

▲ UN peacekeepers have been based in Lebanon since 1978. Here in that year, French troops under the UN mandate set out to patrol villages in south Lebanon that were controlled by the Israeli army.

The United Nations has been involved in peacekeeping for half a century. In 1956, following the Suez invasion, the first UN peacekeeping force monitored the ceasefire and withdrawal of forces from Egypt. Since then, UN peacekeeping activities have increased in number and scope. Until 1988, there were fewer than five UN peacekeeping missions a year, in 1988 there were seven, and in 2006 there were fifteen (see table on page 27).

viewpoints

'The Peacekeeping Forces of the United Nations have, under extremely difficult conditions, contributed to reducing tensions where an armistice has been negotiated but a peace treaty has yet to be established.'
Press release, Nobel Peace Prize, 1988

'Over the years the nickname "blue helmets" has become synonymous with helpless, hapless, lightly armed soldiers from small countries, unable to fire their weapons unless they are under such heavy attack that they will surely be killed anyway.'
Robert Lane Greene, *The Economist Com*, an online current affairs magazine, August 2003

War-torn societies

In the past, UN peacekeeping was largely responsive – monitoring ceasefires, supervising prisoner exchanges and so on. Today, peacekeeping forces do much more – so that they are often described as peacemaking operations. They have become more proactive, protecting civilians, ensuring the delivery of humanitarian aid, preparing for democratic elections, and assisting with the rebuilding of war-torn societies. Most controversially, many have a mandate to use force against those who threaten to break the peace.

There have been several reasons for these changes. The end of the Cold War has meant that the UN itself is less divided and more willing to intervene. Countries in conflict are now more willing to call on the international community for help. The growth of media coverage brings conflict situations on to television screens 24 hours a day, and makes them a major part of political decision-making. Above all, there has been a growing international awareness of past failures to support and protect people in war-torn societies.

Support for peacekeeping

In general, there has been widespread support for UN peacekeeping activities. Peacekeeping missions must be agreed by the UN Security Council and voted on in the General Assembly, the UN's governing body. For this reason, peacekeeping forces are usually seen as neutral and unbiased. The UN has no army of its own, so member countries volunteer forces from their armies and UN members pay for them collectively.

Peacekeeping can be difficult and risky for armies serving a long way from home in countries as diverse as Cyprus, Lebanon, Cambodia, Burundi, Haiti, Liberia, Sierra Leone and the Democratic Republic of Congo. And there have been sacrifices, with more than 2,000 peacekeepers killed in action. Their achievements were recognized when UN peacekeeping forces were awarded the Nobel Peace Prize in 1988.

There are, however, critics of UN military interventions, particularly those that go beyond straightforward tasks such as ceasefire monitoring. Some people see the UN itself as biased. Given that most interventions take place in Africa and the Middle East, the UN is sometimes accused of taking over the role of the old colonial powers, dominating and policing the world's poorest countries. Other critics point out that the UN missions mirror the inequalities in the world, with poor countries such as India, Bangladesh and Pakistan contributing most of the soldiers and with richer countries paying the bills.

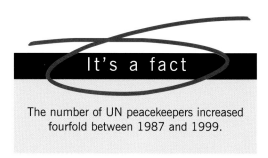

It's a fact

The number of UN peacekeepers increased fourfold between 1987 and 1999.

There is also criticism that the UN system is slow and ineffective. The Security Council must authorize all military interventions. This means it can take a long time to agree and organize the peacekeeping forces. Valuable time is sometimes lost as countries discuss the details. Not all nations are willing to pay their share of the peacekeeping budget, so there is always a financial shortfall.

Critics say that the management of UN operations is inefficient and expensive. Many prefer to see regional organizations, like NATO (North Atlantic Treaty Organization) or the AU (African Union), take on peacekeeping operations in their areas. But these often face similar problems to the UN.

There have been allegations that some UN troops in Europe and Africa have become involved in corrupt activities, such as human trafficking or the abuse of children. (The UN has acknowledged these problems and has taken action to prevent them). At times, UN troops have been accused of cowardice and unwillingness to intervene to stop violence – although their mandate often restricts what they can do. Despite some success, UN peacekeeping reached a crisis in the 1990s. In Somalia, Bosnia and Rwanda, UN forces were seen as failing to stop conflict or protect civilians from slaughter.

case study

Cambodia – the peacekeeper's story

In 1991, the United Nations took on a huge challenge in Cambodia. For the first time, it governed an entire country, while organizing an election for a new democratic government. UN peacekeeping forces had to ensure a secure environment and train Cambodians to defuse some of the millions of landmines that had been laid throughout the country. Almost 16,000 troops and 3,300 police officers from 45 nations took part in the UN mission; 62 of them were killed in the course of duty.

Sergeant Paul Copeland of the Australian army served with the UN peacekeeping mission in Cambodia in 1993. He still has nightmares about an incident that occurred when he was on patrol in the countryside: ' ...this commo [communist soldier] drove down a single-lane road towards me with a 12.7 millimetre, armour-piercing machine-gun pointed at my head ... he had my life in his hands.' At the last minute, the gunman ordered

Copeland off the road, waving his hand. 'The fields were full of landmines but I had to take a chance or have my head blown off.'

Later Copeland almost lost his life in an accident when patrolling on a small country road in Cambodia. His injuries were so severe that he could no longer play a front-line military role. Nevertheless, he later served with the UN peacekeepers who were monitoring the ceasefire in Egypt's Sinai Desert. He was medically discharged from the army in 2001 and now serves as president of the Australian Peacekeepers' Association.

Paul Copeland says: 'I am a strong advocate of peacekeeping. I think if you can prevent war, it is well worth going out there to try and stop it before it starts. If you've seen some of the people that really need a helping hand overseas, it's good to know that you are helping them and providing a better life for them.'

UN peacekeeping missions, July 2006

	Numbers
Peacekeeping operations	15
Countries contributing uniformed staff	109
Uniformed staff	72,983
– Troops	62,965
– Police	7,337
– Military observers	2,681
Civilian staff and volunteers	14,779
Total deaths of UN peacekeepers 1948-2006	2,285

Source: United Nations

Major UN peacekeeping missions, August 2006

Country/territory	Troops	Observers	Others
Burundi	3,387	111	798
Cote d'Ivoire	6,705	188	1,766
Democratic Republic of Congo	15,854	733	4,692
Ethiopia/Eritrea	3,156	213	421
Haiti	6,311	0	2,842
Kosovo	0	37	4,821
Liberia	14,576	207	2,588
Lebanon	1,990	405	-
Sudan	8,895	678	2,700

Source: United Nations

summary

▶ The United Nations has been involved in peacekeeping for over half a century.

▶ Most peacekeeping operations involve monitoring ceasefires and maintaining peace. More recent missions have helped rebuild war-torn countries and oversee elections.

▶ There have been many criticisms of UN peacekeeping missions and attempts to improve and reform them.

▶ Other organizations, such as NATO and the African Union, have also undertaken peacekeeping missions.

▼ UN peacekeeping in Cambodia: Australian General Sanderson, commander of the UN peacekeeping forces (left), confers with Yasushi Akashi, head of the UN provisional authority in Cambodia (right).

CHAPTER 5

Intervening to prevent disaster

As the Cold War drew to an end in the late 1980s, and the USA emerged as the world's only superpower, some thinkers talked of a 'new world order'. One of the most commonly expressed ideas was that military intervention could be used for humanitarian purposes – to deliver aid to starving people, protect safe zones and bring peace to countries in conflict. While some countries wanted intervention through the United Nations, others regarded the UN as weak and divided and supported a dominant role for the USA and its western allies.

A safe haven for the Kurds

One of the first tests of this new humanitarian role came in 1991 in the aftermath of the first Gulf War. During the war, the Kurdish people of northern Iraq had risen up against the Iraqi dictator Saddam Hussein who had killed and abused the Kurds for years. At the end of the war, Saddam remained in power and wanted revenge. Fearing for their lives, the Kurds began a mass trek towards the Turkish border, where they were stranded without food, water or shelter. In response, western countries declared that this area

▼ Fleeing in fear, thousands of Iraqi Kurds make the journey through the mountains to the Iranian border in April 1991.

Somalia, 1992: starving women and children queue at a feeding station. If it had not been for international aid, many more people would have died. But in 1993 the military intervention ended without bringing peace, and the country was left in the hands of warlords.

would become a safe haven. Military forces and aid agencies began to deliver aid and relieve the worst conditions. Later, when the Kurdish refugees returned to northern Iraq, they were to be protected by a no-fly zone, patrolled by the US and UK airforces.

Did the safe haven and no-fly zone really represent a humanitarian intervention? Supporters say that they protected millions of Kurds from slaughter by Saddam Hussein's troops and allowed them to return safely to their homes. Critics says that western leaders had initially been reluctant to assist the Kurds, and the pressure for humanitarian intervention had come from ordinary citizens who had seen the plight of the Kurds featured on nightly news bulletins.

Failure in Somalia

In 1991, the African country of Somalia fell into chaos, fought over by highly armed warlords. Ceasefires were broken, the crops failed and food aid was looted. Soon millions of Somalians were facing starvation. When UN peacekeepers proved unable to stop the looting, the USA announced that it would provide troops to ensure security for the delivery of food aid. 'Operation Restore Hope', under US command, began in late 1992.

But the Somalian warlords turned against the UN and US troops. In October 1993, US troops became involved in a battle with a prominent warlord. The result was that 18 US soldiers died, together with more than 1,000 Somalis, mainly civilians. With public opinion in the USA now against intervention, by the end of 1993 the USA had withdrawn most of its troops, leaving Somalia in the hands of the warlords, without peace or a functioning government.

▲ The war is over, but the pain remains. A Bosnian Muslim prays by the grave of his son, one of the thousands killed in the Bosnian war of 1992-5.

weblinks

For more information about military intervention for humanitarian reasons, go to www.waylinks.co.uk/EthicalDebates/ militaryintervention

The Somalia experience raised many questions. Critics said that rather than supporting earlier UN efforts, Operation Restore Hope had begun too late, after the worst famine had passed. Instead, it had been driven by media coverage that promoted the image of the USA as a powerful but caring nation. Later, the USA was accused of taking sides, in particular of pursuing warlords rather than providing security or encouraging a peaceful settlement.

Limits of humanitarian intervention

In the following years, several conflicts showed clearly the problems of humanitarian intervention. During the three-year Bosnian war (see the case study on pages 4-5), UN troops had been able to deliver aid supplies and negotiate safe passage for refugees but they had not succeeded in stopping the mass killings or the ethnic cleansing. They had

proclaimed a safe haven, but had not protected the inhabitants from shelling, slaughter and rape. They had not ended the armed siege of Sarajevo nor prevented the destruction of the historic city of Mostar. And when the besieging armies had been threatened with air strikes, UN peacekeepers had been kidnapped and held hostage. The stalemate had been broken only by NATO forces, who were not restricted by the limited UN mandate.

There were similar stories from other countries. In Liberia, in West Africa, ruthless warlords fought for control, causing widespread death and destruction and resulting in the displacement of thousands of people. A combined peacekeeping force from West African countries attempted to stop the fighting and protect civilians, but fighting dragged on for years. In neighbouring Sierra Leone, six UN peacekeepers were kidnapped and murdered by rebel forces, who also slaughtered and mutilated many of the civilians there. The rebels were crushed only after intervention by British troops. In the Democratic Republic of Congo, UN forces could do little to protect civilians from the numerous armies fighting across the vast country in the 'African World War' (see the case study on page 16).

Why have there been so many failures? Many critics say that UN peacekeepers are not equipped to deal with dangerous and dirty wars. The UN peacekeepers lack well-trained troops and equipment, they lack money and, above all, they lack a strong mandate to take action. Looking back,

UN Secretary General Kofi Annan said: 'We have in the past prepared for peacekeeping operations with a best-case scenario: The parties sign an agreement, we assume they will honour it, so we send in lightly armed forces to help them.'

However, supporters of UN intervention point out that UN policy is based on decisions agreed by its members. If countries want the UN peacekeepers to support humanitarian operations, then they must be prepared to give the UN more money and a stronger mandate to act effectively, to protect both their own lives and the lives of others.

▼ In August 2003, thousands of refugees fled the fighting near Liberia's capital, Monrovia. A peace agreement between the conflicting forces was policed by UN peacekeepers.

It's a fact

A study in the *British Medical Journal* said that 375 civilian aid workers and UN peacekeepers were killed in conflict areas between 1985 and 1998.

Critics of humanitarian intervention

Is military intervention for humanitarian reasons a realistic goal, either for the UN or other organizations? Opponents say that 'humanitarianism' can act as a cover for other motives. These may be political objectives – to support a friendly government or overthrow an enemy – or they may be economic objectives – to secure resources, such as oil or diamonds. Some critics believe there may be motives based on religious beliefs, for example in the case of a Christian country like the USA intervening in Islamic states.

Aid agencies have also criticized military intervention to support humanitarian aims. They argue that relief and development aid should be delivered in a neutral and unbiased way, so that it reaches the most needy people. When aid is delivered by the military, especially by non-UN forces, then it is inevitably seen as taking sides. In turn, aid workers become associated with the military and are seen as targets by the warring forces.

▼ Government buildings in Pristina, destroyed in the NATO bombing of Kosovo in June 1999.

c a s e   s t u d y

Kosovo – the aid worker's story

In 1999, Kosovo in former Yugoslavia, became the centre of world attention. There was fierce fighting between militias representing Albanians (the majority population) and the Serbian army. Albanian families fled their homes in fear. NATO, representing the USA and Western European nations, announced that it would intervene in a 'humanitarian operation' to protect the Albanians. NATO began an aerial bombing campaign on 24 March.

Seventy-eight days later, the Serbian government agreed to accept NATO's terms and NATO troops entered Kosovo. Huge numbers of refugees returned to Kosovo to find their homes and communities destroyed by competing militias and by NATO bombing.

Sarah, a British aid worker, was employed by an international charity assisting Kosovo refugees who had sought shelter in neighbouring Macedonia. She found many aspects of the situation very troubling.

'As aid workers we are supposed to be neutral but in Kosovo and Macedonia it looked as though our role was to support the military. In Macedonia NATO troops were everywhere. They designed and built refugee camps, and sometimes provided food and medicines –

work we would normally do. Aid agencies who wanted to work in the camps needed first to request permission from the military commanders.'

'When the NATO troops entered Kosovo, the aid agencies followed a few days later. We relied on the NATO troops to provide security so we could deliver aid to refugees. The roads were often dangerous and there were hidden landmines everywhere. But it looked as through the aid agencies were there to support the NATO troops – especially troops from our own countries. The Serbs especially thought we favoured the Albanians, although we tried to reach out to both sides. We did some good work in Kosovo but we should have kept our distance from the military.'

▼ An aid worker with refugees.

s u m m a r y

▶ The end of the Cold War saw the development of the idea of 'humanitarian' intervention to protect vulnerable people.

▶ UN intervention in Somalia, Bosnia and other countries showed the limits and problems of humanitarian intervention, especially when UN

peacekeepers do not have a strong mandate to act or the necessary resources to support their intervention.

▶ Aid agencies say that military intervention for humanitarian reasons may put their workers in danger.

CHAPTER 6

When there is no intervention

What happens when there is no military intervention? In April 1994, the small African country of Rwanda plunged into a frenzy of killing. Some of the leaders of the majority Hutu tribe, organized in the Interahamwe forces (meaning 'those who fight together'), began to slaughter the minority Tutsi tribe.

The killings spread quickly. In the space of just three months, around one million people were murdered – shot, burned and hacked to death. Women and girls were raped and mutilated. The killings ended only when a Tutsi opposition army defeated the Interahamwe and took over the government.

Genocide and the UN

The killings in Rwanda were so dreadful in their extent and numbers that they were soon recognized as genocide. More than 130 countries have signed the Genocide Convention, which states that: 'Any Contracting Party may call upon the competent organs of the United Nations to take such action... as they consider appropriate for the prevention and suppression of acts of genocide.... '

So why did the UN and its members not intervene to stop the killings? There was already a small UN peacekeeping force in Rwanda, as well as some French troops. In early 1994, the UN Commander, Canadian General Romeo Dallaire, had warned of the potential for mass violence but the UN refused to let him confiscate weapons or give him extra troops. When ten Belgian peacekeepers were murdered in Rwanda the Belgian government withdrew all its troops. Some European governments sent soldiers, but only to evacuate their citizens.

▼ Rwanda genocide: two sisters survive after being hacked on the neck and left for dead for a week, until rescued by their father in May 1994.

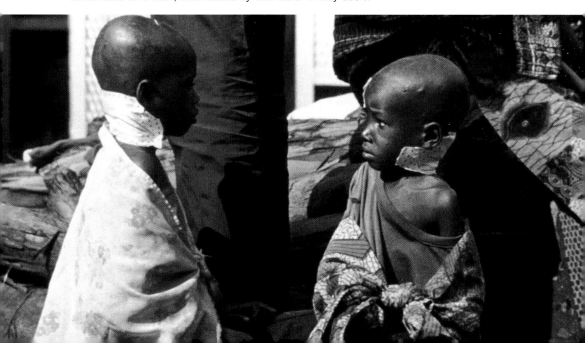

▲ Cambodia: a sea of skulls, victims of the genocide carried out by the Khmer Rouge, a fanatical militia who took over the country in 1975, killing and starving 1.7 million people in four years.

At first, the UN Security Council refused to help. Russia, France and China declared that the matter was an 'internal affair' and the USA refused to supply troops or equipment. After the failure of the US military intervention in Somalia 18 months earlier, President Bill Clinton was determined that he would not place US troops at risk in another dangerous and unpredictable African conflict.

Instead of sending reinforcements, the Security Council decided to reduce the numbers of peacekeepers in Rwanda from 2,000 to just 260. This tiny force did its best against terrible odds and is credited with saving 20,000 lives. But around them, the slaughter continued.

weblinks

For more information about humanitarian emergencies worldwide, go to www.waylinks.co.uk/EthicalDebates/militaryintervention

It's a fact

The Genocide Convention grew out of a determination to prevent deliberate mass killings like the Nazi Holocaust of the Jews during the Second World War. It was adopted by the United Nations in 1948 and came into effect in 1951.

Too little too late

Unlike the continuing conflict in Bosnia, Rwanda received little media attention and there was little public pressure for governments to take action. When the UN did react, it was slow and indecisive. At the end of April 1994, the UN stated that 'acts of genocide might have been committed' and agreed to send 5,000 UN peacekeepers, mainly from African countries. However, there was disagreement over the cost, and UN forces did not arrive in Rwanda until after the genocide had ended.

When the killings started, General Dallaire had urged the UN to give him 4,000 troops, as he believed that a small force would be able to stop the killings in the first days. But would such a small force have been adequate? The Interahamwe killers were well prepared, they had stockpiled weapons and they used their own radio station to spread hatred against the Tutsis. Critics say that even a larger force would not have been effective – at best it might have slowed the killings or reduced the numbers killed. They point out that the genocide progressed so quickly – half a million were killed in the first month – that it would not have been possible to assemble a UN force in time to make a difference.

▼ After their defeat in Rwanda, many Hutus fled into the neighbouring country of Zaire. Here French troops search people for weapons as they cross the border.

▲ The UN Security Council must approve all military interventions. Here members vote on action against Iraq in November 1990.

However, supporters of intervention argue that the international community has an obligation to act in situations of genocide. They say that early and forceful military intervention would not only have stopped most of the killings but would also have delivered a message to the perpetrators that such actions would not be tolerated.

weblinks▸

For more information about United Nations policy-making, go to www.waylinks.co.uk/EthicalDebates/militaryintervention

It's a fact

The International Criminal Court (ICC) was established in 2002 as a permanent tribunal to prosecute individuals for genocide, crimes against humanity and war crimes. By July 2006, 101 countries had approved the ICC Statute – exceptions included the USA and many Asian and African countries.

Darfur, Sudan – the campaigner's story

During the Rwanda genocide in 1994, Paul Rusesabagina was the manager of one of the country's best hotels. With a mixture of courage and cunning, Rusesabagina not only saved the lives of his family but also those of the 1,200 desperate people who took shelter in his hotel. His story was later told in the film *Hotel Rwanda*.

Today Paul Rusesabagina continues to speak out for the victims of genocide. He is now campaigning for the displaced people of Darfur, a vast desert region in western Sudan.

▲ Paul Rusesabagina today.

When Paul Rusesabagina visited Darfur in 2005, he said: 'What I saw was exactly what I saw in Rwanda.... There were government-funded helicopters destroying villages. Militia armed by the government killing villagers. Two million people displaced and their homes completely erased.'

In 2004, the African Union (AU), an organization of African countries, agreed to provide peacekeeping troops, with support from the United Nations. Despite constant obstruction by the Sudanese government, AU forces had increased in number to almost 7,000 by July 2006. However, plans to hand over peacekeeping to a larger UN force were blocked by the Sudanese government.

The conflict in Darfur started in early 2003 with an uprising by local tribes against the dictatorial Sudanese government. In retaliation, the government supported tribal militias, the Janjaweed, taking revenge on the rebels and the local population. The results were disastrous. Millions of people were driven from their homes; their villages were burned and bombed and their crops were destroyed.

Many people took shelter in refugee camps, living on rations from aid agencies. However, the camps were unsafe, raided by the Janjaweed who regularly murdered and raped women and girls. By 2006, at least 400,000 people had been killed by the Janjaweed or had died from starvation. Many people saw this process as a genocide.

Paul Rusesabagina says that the AU troops have been unable to stop the genocide. 'They lack helicopters, jeeps and firepower and they lack a sense of purpose.' Instead he wants to see intervention by the UN. He says: 'The UN Security Council must create a tool that it has lacked for far too long – a small multinational rapid response force which can quickly airlift tanks, jeeps, helicopters and troops to spots where the evidence of genocide is overwhelming.'

The 'responsibility to protect'

There has since been huge criticism of the inaction of the UN, and especially its leading members for their indecision and unwillingness to intervene in Rwanda. An independent enquiry, issued in 1999, found that the UN had ignored evidence that genocide was planned and refused to act once it had begun.

One of the outcomes of this enquiry was an impetus for the UN to monitor and react to situations of genocide. In September 2005, the UN General Assembly accepted that it had 'the responsibility to protect populations from genocide, war crimes, ethnic cleansing and crimes against humanity', if necessary by the use of force. But this still has to be put into practice, as can be seen in the situation in Darfur (see case study opposite).

summary

▶ There was no UN military intervention to stop the 1994 genocide in Rwanda; the UN reduced the number of peacekeepers and was slow to respond.

▶ There is debate about whether UN intervention would have been quick or effective enough to stop the genocide in Rwanda.

▶ The UN failure in Rwanda led to the UN accepting a new principle of 'responsibility to protect'.

▶ Some people believe that the international community is failing to protect the people of Darfur in western Sudan.

▲ A Rwandan soldier (left) is instructed by a Canadian soldier (right) at a Canadian-led training course for the African Union peacekeeping force in Darfur in western Sudan. By mid-2006, there were 7,000 African Union peacekeepers in Darfur.

CHAPTER 7

The costs of intervention

▲ Burnt-out cars symbolize the devastation of the first Gulf War of 1991.

The strongest argument against military intervention is the simplest – it kills people and destroys communities. But supporters reply that, whatever the costs, military intervention ultimately saves and protects lives too.

The casualties

Even the most carefully planned methods of military intervention cost lives. Troops on both sides die in action or from 'friendly fire', but most of the casualties are civilians, especially the most vulnerable people – such as babies, children, the sick and the elderly. The destruction of roads and transport, hospitals and health centres means that people are more likely to die of their injuries. Damage to electricity and water supplies can spread disease and make people's lives difficult for months, or years to come.

Supporters of military action point out that today's sophisticated warfare is more precise than it used to be. It produces fewer military and civilian casualties and less random destruction. Satellites can pinpoint military targets and direct aerial bombs with greater precision. Similarly, with night-vision equipment, soldiers can provide round-the-clock security.

However, critics say that even with careful planning errors occur, resulting in huge numbers of civilian casualties that are often ignored and uncounted. Cluster bombs (bombs containing smaller bomblets designed to cause greater damage) and bombs containing radioactive depleted uranium can cause long-term damage, while the psychological distress and noise from constant bombing can traumatize survivors. In any case, some of the most destructive wars of recent times, such as the one in the Democratic Republic of Congo, have been fought largely with relatively simple weapons, such as machine guns and machetes.

The after effects

Critics also point out that not all instances of military intervention are successful. For example, the US military action against al-Qaeda in Afghanistan did not destroy the organization or its leaders and may have inspired others to join a revived al-Qaeda organization. Similarly, UN peacekeeping operations, like those in Croatia and Bosnia, failed to stop ethnic cleansing or mass killings.

Even when interventions are successful in military terms, they can have unforeseen results for years ahead. Fighting emphasizes winners and losers with the result that already fragile societies are shattered, divisions between ethnic and religious groups are deepened and political reconciliation becomes more difficult.

Supporters claim that military intervention can create security out of chaos. Sometimes, safety and security do improve, especially where UN or other international peacekeeping forces are providing support for rebuilding and for the implementation of a democratic political process. Peacekeeping can only go so far – to be successful it needs long-term commitment on all sides. And, since the countries involved are often very poor, they will need economic support for many years to come. In practice, this support is rarely forthcoming. Donor countries may break their promises or shift support elsewhere after a few years.

Critics point out that military interventions are often ill-judged and carried out in haste, without thought for the longer-term consequences. For example, the Iraq invasion of 2003 did result in the overthrow of a dictatorial regime, but it was replaced by a divided and chaotic society, where violent deaths became an everyday occurrence, leading many Iraqis to hate and despise their 'liberators'.

▼ Military intervention can unleash long-held hatreds, increase opposition and create insecurity. This photo below shows the aftermath of one of many suicide bombings in Iraq, 2006.

▲ Civilians flee their homes in south Beirut, Lebanon. In August 2006 the country was subjected to a bombing campaign by the Israeli army. Around 1,500 people were killed and 900,000 Lebanese were forced to flee for their lives.

Unexpected effects

Even well-intentioned military interventions, such as UN peacekeeping missions, can have unexpected effects. Young soldiers, far from home, may be drawn into prostitution and drug trafficking. There is usually a big income gap between the troops and local people, and the presence of large numbers of military personnel places strains on local resources and drives up prices. In the longer term, already weak economies may become dependent on outside aid. Once the peacekeepers are withdrawn, the old divisions and tensions may resurface.

Alternative action

Is military intervention the best way to solve international problems? Many people feel that it should only be used as a last resort and other methods should be considered first. Where a country breaks international law or abuses human rights, other countries could use diplomatic pressure, for example by denying visas to government officials, stopping cultural exchanges or withdrawing economic aid. Critics say that such measures have little impact on a dictatorial government – and may just leave the country itself more isolated and withdrawn.

Similarly, diplomatic pressure can try to resolve conflicts by encouraging the warring sides to negotiate. But this is a long process, and even if agreement is reached, low-level warfare usually continues away from the negotiating table. Often agreements need outside peacekeeping forces to monitor the ceasefire and ensure that disarmament takes place.

Another option is the introduction of international economic sanctions, usually imposed through the United Nations. Sanctions are economic boycotts. They may be broad-ranging (for example, banning all goods going into or coming out of a country) or they may be limited to just a few items (such as oil or diamonds). Between 1949 and 1994, when South Africa maintained an apartheid system which denied black people their human rights and treated them as inferior to white people, many countries imposed economic sanctions to force change.

Critics say that sanctions often have little effect, especially on stronger economies, and can be cruel and indiscriminate in their impact. Critics argue that sanctions fail to punish dictatorial governments, but encourage corruption instead. While the richest people buy banned goods on the black market (this is against the law), the poorest people go without essential items, such as medicines. Critics point to the disastrous effects of UN sanctions on Iraq – the so-called 'oil for food' programme – which plunged the majority of Iraqis into poverty, while allowing corrupt officials to make huge profits.

The supporters of military intervention point out that alternatives can take a long time to have an effect and may be ignored by governments. For example, would diplomatic pressure or economic sanctions have stopped the genocide in Rwanda? Sometimes, they argue, military intervention may be the only effective way to stop slaughter and protect civilians.

But, as the *Human Security Report* points out, the most effective interventions are those that prevent wars and conflicts from happening in the first place. These can range from global human rights initiatives, like the new International Criminal Court, to local peacemaking activities, for example, by bringing young people from different communities together to help build trust and co-operation.

▼ Sanctions that are intended to punish a government often severely affect the lives of ordinary people. Here Iraqis protest against UN sanctions outside the UN headquarters in Baghdad in 1993.

In the long term, people need economic and political security. Today, many of the most destructive wars are fought over scarce resources in the poorest countries. Supporting policies that enable the people to have jobs, education and a good standard of living, as citizens in a democratic country, leads to a more secure world for everyone.

Will we ever live in a completely peaceful world? Probably not – there will always be tensions between countries and some governments will continue to abuse their people. The challenge in the twenty-first century is to seek ways in which to resolve conflicts peacefully and effectively, without resorting to military intervention.

It's a fact

In October 2006, 139 members of the UN General Assembly voted in favour of a treaty to control international trade in conventional weapons, ranging from guns to tanks. However, the treaty will not come into force until 2009 or later.

'War can seriously damage your health': anti-war advertisements were part of the efforts to enforce a ceasefire in Macedonia in August 2001.

WARNING: WAR CAN SERIOUSLY DAMAGE YOUR HEALTH

case study

Macedonia – the journalist's story

In 2001, the majority Macedonian and minority Albanian communities in the small country of Macedonia in south-eastern Europe seemed to be on the verge of civil war.

Ana Petruseva, a journalist based in Skopje, Macedonia's capital, looks back. 'The year 2001 was supposed to be a good year for Macedonia. Talks with the European Union (EU) were underway and there were solid chances for economic revival. That all ended when the minority Albanians suddenly began an armed struggle for greater civil rights against a state they saw as oppressive. But as the government proved unable to handle the crisis, the international community became increasingly involved, determined to prevent another hotspot developing in the Balkans.'

When fighting erupted in the hills above Skopje, the government asked NATO to send troops to disarm the Albanian militias. NATO agreed, but only on the condition that the government and rebels negotiate a ceasefire and reach a peaceful settlement. An agreement of August 2001 stated that Albanians would have more rights while, in return, the Albanian militias would cease fighting and hand their weapons over to NATO.

NATO agreed to monitor the disarmament process and sent 3,500 troops from fifteen countries to Macedonia. Most of the weapons were handed over in the first month. A smaller NATO force remained to oversee elections in 2002.

Ana Petruseva says: 'Since the signing of the Ohrid Agreement, inter-ethnic relations have gradually improved. That does not change the fact that Macedonian and Albanian communities remain divided. But there is little danger now of a new war. The European Union is where Macedonia sees its future.'

summary

▶ In all military interventions there are death and injury to people and damage to facilities.

▶ Supporters of military intervention say that today more precise and sophisticated warfare helps to minimize loss, but critics say that errors still occur and it is impossible to calculate long-term consequences.

▶ There are alternatives to military intervention, such as diplomatic pressure and trade sanctions, but these can take a long time and are not always effective.

▶ We need to develop non-military alternatives to support a fairer and more peaceful world.

Glossary

African Union (AU) An international organization of 53 African member states, founded in July 2002.

Capitalist A system of government where most resources are in private hands (of individuals or companies).

Civilians People not involved in fighting, non-combatants.

Coalition A group of countries that join forces, working to an agreed objective; or a group of political parties that join together on a common programme.

Colonial A system of governing one colony or a group of colonies.

Colony Territory seized (often by force) or owned by another country.

Communist A person who believes in a system of government where the state owns all or most resources, and power is in the hands of one party, the Communist Party.

Coup The overthrow of a government by military action.

Disproportionate Describes a response which is carried out with far greater force than is necessary.

Ethnic cleansing The forcible removal of members of an ethnic group from their homes – used in Balkan wars in 1991-95.

Ethnic group People of the same skin colour, social background, language.

European Union (EU) A political and economic union of 25 European countries, established under this name in 1992.

Friendly fire An attack made in error by a country's own troops or those of its allies.

Genocide Actions intended to destroy, in whole or in part, a national, ethnic or religious group.

Guerrilla warfare Fighting or harassment by small independent groups of fighters.

Indigenous Originating in a country or region.

International missions Peacekeeping missions led by the UN or international alliances such as NATO. International missions are made up of regular armies of member countries and often have a very limited mandate.

Mandate An authority to perform agreed tasks – for example, for forces to protect refugees or attack under certain conditions.

Militia An informal military force, usually made up of non-professional soldiers.

NATO (North Atlantic Treaty Organization) A military alliance of the USA, Canada and European countries, currently with 26 members, founded in 1949.

Negotiated settlement An international agreement to end warfare, signed by warring sides.

No-fly zones Areas where hostile aircraft are banned and may be shot down. No-fly zones are often linked to safe havens and are designed to stop aerial bombing of civilians.

Pre-emptive Describes the taking of action before something happens – sometimes referred to as 'preventative'.

Proxy war A war in which an army (either of a country or an opposition group) fights on behalf of another country, usually in a secretive way. Also called 'stealth war'.

Refugee A person fleeing war or political or religious persecution.

Safe haven An area where people (inhabitants or refugees) are protected from attack by military force.

Sanctions Punishment, specifically a boycott of goods and services.

Security Council A UN body with prime responsibility for maintaining international peace and security. It has five permanent members (China, France, Russia, the UK and USA) and ten temporary elected members.

Siege The surrounding and blockading of a place by armed forces in order to capture it.

Timeline

1945 Foundation of the United Nations (UN), initially with 51 members (today 192 members).

1948 Universal Declaration of Human Rights. UN Truce Supervision Organization established.

1949 Establishment of North Atlantic Treaty Organization (NATO) by USA, Canada and many western European countries.

1956 UK, France and Israel invade Egypt (Suez crisis); first UN peacekeeping force sent to monitor ceasefire and withdrawal of forces. Soviet Union invades Hungary.

1965-75 Vietnam War, with massive US military intervention.

1975-79 Khmer Rouge takes power in Cambodia and commits mass killings; overthrown by Vietnam invasion of 1979.

1990-91 Iraq invades Kuwait, followed by First Gulf War as UN coalition forces invade Iraq; Kurdish refugees flee to Turkish border and are protected in coalition safe haven.

1991-93 UN peacekeeping operation in Cambodia, administering democratic elections and overseeing mine clearance.

1991-94 Civil war and famine in Somalia leads to UN and US intervention; continued warfare sees Somalia remain as a 'failed state'.

1991-95 War and ethnic cleansing in former Yugoslavia, especially Bosnia, shows weak mandate of UN peacekeeping forces.

1994 Rwanda genocide – UN does not act to prevent genocide of Tutsi population.

1999 NATO intervenes in Kosovo and Serbia; later Kosovo is placed under UN 'protectorship'.

1998-2003 'African World War' in the Democratic Republic of Congo; UN peacekeeping mission later strengthens its mandate and increases troop numbers.

2000 Civil war in Sierra Leone results in UK military intervention.

2001 9/11 (11 September) al-Qaeda terrorist attacks in USA; followed by US military intervention against al-Qaeda in Afghanistan, leading to fall of Taliban government; UN and NATO forces remain to support new government.

2003 US, UK and a 'coalition of the willing' invade Iraq in March; three weeks later they declare victory in Baghdad as Saddam Hussein's regime collapses. In the following years there is a huge increase in killings and insecurity.

2003 UN peacekeepers in Liberia oversee ceasefire and support peace process.

2003-06 African Union peacekeepers in Darfur, western Sudan, despite opposition from Sudanese government.

2006 UN peacekeepers support democratic elections in Democratic Republic of the Congo.

Further information

http://www.globalpolicy.org/

The Global Policy Forum is an independent organization monitoring United Nations policy-making.

http://www.humansecurityreport.info

The *Human Security Report 2005* with facts and figures on conflicts worldwide.

http://www.iciss.ca

The Independent International Commission on Intervention and State Sovereignty Report on the 'Responsibility to Protect', commissioned by the Canadian government.

http://www.bbc.co.uk/worldservice/people /features/ihavearightto/four_b/casestudy_art2 8.shtml

I have a right to... military intervention for human rights – part of a BBC World Service series on the UN and human rights.

http://www.responsibilitytoprotect.org

Explains the principle of 'responsibility to protect' against genocide and human rights abuses, with information about the situation in Darfur.

http://www.iwpr.net

The Institute for War and Peace Reporting has reports by local journalists on conflicts around the world.

Index

Numbers in **bold** refer to
illustrations.

African Union (AU) 26, 38, **39**
aid workers 33, **33**
al-Qaeda **18**, 19, 20, 21, 41
Annan, Kofi 31
anti-war protests **23**
apartheid 43

bin Laden, Osama 19
Blair, Prime Minister Tony 21
Bosnia-Herzegovina 4-5, **5**, 30,
    30, 41
Bush, President George W. 19,
    21, 22

Cambodia 26, **27**, **35**
capitalism 12-13
casualties of war 5, 12, 16, 17, **20**,
    22, 31, 40
child soldiers 16, 17, **17**
civilians 20, 23, 26, 31, 40, **42**
Clinton, President Bill 35
Cold War, the 12-13, **12-13**, 14, 17
colonies 12
communism 12-13, 15, **15**, 26
corruption 26, 43
coups 14, **14**, 15
Croatia 4, 41

Dallaire, General Romeo 34, 36
Darfur 38, **39**
Democratic Republic of Congo 16,
    16, 31, 41
diplomacy 42

ethnic cleansing 4, 30, 39, 41
ethnic groups 4, 45

famine 11, 16, 30

genocide 6, 11, 34-9, **35**
Genocide Convention 34, 35
Genghis Khan **10**

guerrillas 9, 14, 20
Gulf War 28, **40**

humanitarian intervention 4, 28-33
human rights 22, 42, 43
Hussein, Saddam 21, **21**, 22, 28

Interhamwe 34-6
International Criminal Court (ICC)
    37, 43
international law 6, 7, 42

Janjaweed 38

Kurds 28-9, **28**

landmines 26, 33

Macedonia **44**, 45
military intervention
    consequences of 41-2, **41**
    in Afghanistan 19, **19**, 20, **20**, 41
    in Angola **15**
    in Bosnia 4-5, **5**, 30
    in Chechnya **7**, 19
    in Cyprus **9**
    in Egypt **12**, 13
    in Guatemala **14**
    in Hungary 13, **13**
    in Iraq 6, **6**, 19, 21, 22, 23,
        23, 41
    in Lebanon **24**, **42**
    in Liberia 30, **31**
    in Kosovo **32**, 33, **33**
    in Sierra Leone 30-31
    in Somalia 29-30, **29**
militias 16, 33, 38, 45
MONUC 16

national security 18-19
neo-conservatives 7, 15
no-fly zones 29
North Atlantic Treaty Organization
    (NATO) 19, 26, 30, **32**,
    33, 45

pacifists 6
proxy wars 14, **14**, 15, **15**

refugees 4, **31**, 33
rogue states 7
Rusesabagina, Paul 38, **38**
Rwanda 6, **8**, 34-6, **34**, 38, 39

safe havens 4-5, 29, 30
sanctions 7, 42-3, **43**
Serbia 4
Suez crisis **12**, 13, 24

Taliban, the 19, 20, 21
terrorism 7, 18-19, **18**, 20, 21
trade routes 12, 13
troops
    Australian 26, **27**
    British **12**, 31
    Russian **7**
    US **6**, **19**, 22, 29

United Nations (UN) 4, 6, 7, 11, 12,
    16, 22, 24-7, 28, 30, 34, 35, 36,
    39, 43
    General Assembly 25, 39, 44
    inspectors 21
    peacekeepers 4, **5**, **9**, **16**, 24,
        24, 25-7, **27**, 29, 30, 31, 34, 35,
        36, 38, 41, 42
    Protection Force (UNPROFOR)
        4-5
    Security Council 9, 25, 26, 35,
        37, 38

'war on terror' 19, **19**, 20, **20**
wars 8-9, 10. 12, 16, 17, 29, 30, **30**,
    31, 38, 41, 44, **44**
weapons of mass destruction
    (WMDs) 21, 22

ETHICAL DEBATES

Contents of titles in the series:

MILITARY INTERVENTION 978 07502 5028 3

Introduction: Real-life case study
1. What is military intervention?
2. The reasons for military intervention
3. Defending national security
4. Intervening to keep the peace
5. Intervening to prevent disaster
6. When there is no intervention
7. The costs of intervention

TERRORISM 978 07502 5029 0

Introduction: Real-life case study
1. Different kinds of terrorism
2. Terrorism tactics in wartime
3. Terrorism tactics in peacetime
4. Counter-terrorism and human rights
5. Terrorism and international law
6. The impact of the War on Terror
7. Terrorism in the twenty-first century

IMMIGRATION 978 07502 5027 6

Introduction: Real-life case study
1. What is immigration?
2. The history of immigration
3. Is immigration out of control?
4. How immigration affects the host economy
5. The effects of immigration
6. Controlling immigration
7. Does immigration cause racism?
8. Does immigration benefit society?

THE DEATH PENALTY 978 07502 5024 5

Introduction: Real-life case study
1. What is the death penalty?
2. Is the death penalty ever justified?
3. Death – the final reckoning
4. Can the death penalty ever be humane?
5. Who dies and who lives?
6. Does the death penalty make
   society safer?
7. The death penalty and society

GLOBALIZATION 978 07502 5025 2

Introduction: Real-life case study
1. The global village
2. Trade, wealth and poverty
3. The politics of globalization
4. Planetary matters
5. Globalization and its opponents

GENETIC ENGINEERING 978 07502 5026 9

Introduction: Real-life case study
1. From genius to genes
2. Agriculture
3. Medicine
4. Designing babies
5. Forensics and crime scenes
6. The wider uses of genetic engineering
7. Finance and Future